C0-DXE-628

The Journal of a Woman with *Lived* Experiences

A 21-Day Guided Journal

SHAWNTA JACKSON

Copyright

Copyright © 2019 by Shawnta Jackson. All rights reserved.

Published by Shawnta Jackson, Riverdale, MD.

No part of this book may be reproduced or transmitted in any form or by any means, electronic or mechanical, including photocopying, recording or by any information storage and retrieval system, without written permission from the author, except for the inclusion of brief quotations embodied in critical articles, reviews and testimonials. Requests should be emailed to inquiries@shawntajackson.com.

This book may be purchased for educational or promotional use. For more information, please email inquiries@shawntajackson.com.

This book contains information and education related to health care, psychology, social and behavioral health, and intimate relationships. It should be used as an informative guide and should not replace the advice of a licensed health care provider, clinician or trained health professional, counselor, coach or safety officer. The information in this book is based on the author's research, interpretations, opinions and experience which may not agree with other interpretations and conclusions. All efforts have been made to assure accuracy of the information contained in this book as of the date of publication. The author disclaims liability for any medical outcomes that may occur as a result of applying the methods suggested in this book.

Shawnta Jackson

The Journal of a Woman with Lived Experiences: A 21-Day Guided Journal.

ISBN: 978-1-54399-970-9

Printed in the United States of America

Dedication

To all women with lived experiences

Contents

Introduction ix

1st Journal Entry *Owning Your Story: The Power of Storytelling* 1

2nd Journal Entry *Positive Affirmations* 11

3rd Journal Entry *Expressions of Gratitude* 17

4th Journal Entry *Manifesting Love* 23

5th Journal Entry *Expecting Love* 29

6th Journal Entry *Self-Validation* 33

7th Journal Entry *Depending on a Power Greater Than Yourself* 39

8th Journal Entry *Allowing Yourself to Trust Someone Else* 45

9th Journal Entry *Balancing Independence and Relationships* 51

10th Journal Entry *Unconditional Love and Commitment* 57

11th Journal Entry *Shallow Thinking* 63

12th Journal Entry *Staying True to Yourself* 69

13th Journal Entry *Managing Anxiety and Stress* 75

14th Journal Entry *Your Relationship with Time and Money* 81

15th Journal Entry *Spontaneous Thoughts* 87

16th Journal Entry *Life in the Present Moment* 93

17th Journal Entry *Life Visioning* 99

18th Journal Entry *Another Expression of Gratitude* 105

19th Journal Entry *Striving for Success* 111

20th Journal Entry *Perseverance* 117

21st Journal Entry *Life's Bucket List* 123

About the Author 131

References 133

INTRODUCTION

Thank you for taking the time to explore this guided journal and for giving me the opportunity to share my most intimate and critical thoughts. I'm nervous and a little embarrassed, but I decided to move forward with this project because I want to take a chance on myself. I like to believe that this journal will get in the hands of those who will benefit from it the most.

You and I are going to walk through this journal together. I'm sharing expressions that I wrote in my personal journal and I'm encouraging you to write your thoughts as you read through my entries. While I'm not a psychologist or licensed counselor, I'm a woman with lived experiences and thoughts that may be beneficial and help you to organize your thoughts about yourself, your relationships, your choices, and how you process your emotions.

What I'm sharing with you are my personal journal entries that served as moments of reflection, clarity, venting, affirmation, prayer, planning, and gratitude. Usually, once I finish a journal, I throw it away out of shame and embarrassment, but this time I had a vision to share what I wrote in an effort to help someone else. And maybe, that's you.

If you decide to fully participate with this form of self-reflection, you too may feel embarrassed or ashamed of your thoughts and actions, and that's okay. We are only human and it's better to exercise some form of self-reflection and self-care rather than live in a state of low self-awareness, bitterness, ungratefulness, denial, and stress.

These will be your thoughts and you have the right to throw this journal away like I've done in the past, and you also have the right to share with others, just as I'm sharing with you in this moment.

The intended benefits of using this 21-day guided journal include:

- Clarification of your thoughts and feelings
- A better personal understanding of yourself
- Relief from stress and anxiety
- An increase in your problem-solving skills
- An improvement in the way you communicate with the people who matter
- Other positive impacts on your physical and mental well-being

1st JOURNAL ENTRY

Owning your Story: The Power of Storytelling

As humans, we all face some type of adversity in our lives and as hard as it seems in the moment and even after, we are resilient. I'm resilient. You're resilient.

The purpose of this first journal entry is to help you understand the importance of telling and owning your personal story as a way to help yourself and others. Telling your story also helps you to find peace within and establishes your voice. Be heard!

I'll begin with one of my stories of resilience that I consider a turning point in my life.

Shawnta's 1st Journal Entry

Owning Her Story: The Power of Storytelling

For a long time, I suppressed (almost forgot) my memories and past—those same memories and the past are also a testament to my strength. The same memories and past that molded me into the person I am today. The same memories and past that help me understand, motivate, and help others. They are the same memories and past that have helped me to know and understand myself.

When I was nineteen, I fell in love with a guy who had five children. I met him during the second semester of my freshman year of college. We had not planned it that way, but I ended up moving in with him that summer. The original plan was for me to go home to Las Vegas and spend time with my family and then stay with him in Chicago until school started again. I was then going to get an apartment with two girls from New York. Long story short, my whole family acted like I was running away when I flew back to Chicago to stay with him. Out of rebellion, I stayed. I was super in love, too.

He and I lived together for two years before we got married. Before we were married, I recall him hitting me on three different occasions. When we were married, I was still in college and twenty-one years old at the time. Two years later, I had my son. When I was pregnant, he slapped me so hard that I landed on the floor with my nose bleeding. Almost two years after that, we were divorced. Over the course of the years that we were together, we had good moments and he was a good provider, but it was an unhealthy relationship. He was the only person who could treat me so well *and* so bad at the same time.

Toward the end of our relationship, I was on the phone with a girlfriend and my husband overheard me say something that upset him. He pulled the phone cord out of the wall in the middle of my conversation and then cornered me in the bathroom and said he would beat me until I was black and blue. That day, I sat outside with my son for hours until he left the house.

The first time that I left him was when he hit me when I was pregnant. I was never going to let him see our son and I took fifty percent of the money that was in the bank. He never knew any of this because I ended up redepositing the money and going back to him after staying with friends for a few days.

Fast forward to the end of this story (yes, I'm rushing through it because it is hard to tell). It was about two weeks before my son's first birthday. We took a road trip with my husband's mom and two of his daughters to Atlanta for his grandmother's birthday. The girls stayed with his mom and my son and I stayed with him at his uncle's house. I'll never forget how he treated me. He left me alone, talked down to me, and slapped me while I was holding my son. He was also on the phone with his mother when this happened. After he slapped me, my son emulated him and hit me too.

On our way back to Chicago, I rode in the back of the minivan with my stepdaughters. His mom was driving. When we stopped to get gas I figured he and I could switch seats, so I hopped in the front passenger seat and as if I were a child, he gestured his hand in a shoo motion and asked me what I was doing and told me to go to the backseat. Before I knew it, I looked at him and said, "Fuck you." This wasn't a regular "fuck you." This was an *I'm finished* "fuck you."

At that point, he had an uncontrollable fit. He called me all kinds of names and talked to me so badly that everyone in the car was crying except for my son and me. I called my mom who stayed on the phone with me for a while; she kept telling me not to say anything to him.

I had $200 in cash hidden in my sunglasses case. All I needed was to get close enough to Chicago to catch a cab to the airport. Coincidentally, I had a pre-booked plane ticket for later that day to Las Vegas so that I could prepare for my son's first birthday party with my family.

We stopped at a restaurant in Anytown USA (maybe Indiana) and I had to ask him for money to buy his daughters something to eat. I could not let him know that I had money on me because he would have taken it. While he was outside with his mom, his daughters and I sat at a table after we ordered and the oldest, who was about eleven years old at the time, said that if she were me, she would leave. She told me that he did the same thing to her "mommy."

When we arrived at his mom's house, I was still not able to call a cab. I had to keep asking his mom to take me to the airport. She tried to avoid me. He then chased me around the minivan and around the house because I refused to leave with him. He had hit me before, but he had never repeatedly beaten me, and I knew that would change if I got in the minivan with him. All I could think of was one of those *Lifetime* movies. I just knew that we would die in a car crash with my baby in the car.

His mom eventually drove me and my son to the airport. I had the $200, a baby, a car seat, and three pairs of dirty clothes from the trip to Atlanta. I never had the opportunity to go back to my home. I left tax documents, my Social Security card, baby pictures, clothes, jewelry, and more. I literally left my house one day and never went back.

My son's first birthday was two weeks later. Our wedding anniversary was the next day. Pre-Atlanta, we had planned for my son's party to take place in Las Vegas and for us to go to Hawaii the next day. We did everything as planned. My husband flew to Las Vegas and we celebrated my son's first birthday with all of my family in my mom's backyard. At that moment, I was still wearing my wedding ring and smiling. I remember wearing an orange top and gold chandelier earrings. I am not sure who in my family knew what had happened just a few weeks before and honestly, I think that I was already starting to forgive him.

After Hawaii, he went back to Chicago and I stayed in Las Vegas for about six months. I ended up filing for divorce and during those six months started dating someone else. But somehow, my then estranged husband and I ended up on the phone one day and decided to try again. We agreed that he would come to Las Vegas and we would go out on a date. However, the day he arrived in Las Vegas, he greeted me unannounced while I was asleep in my bedroom at my mother's house. I woke up to find him standing over me. That's when I knew that he was really crazy, but instead of acting startled, I controlled the situation and immediately greeted him with a smile.

After his arrival, we spent more time together and he moved to Las Vegas and without my knowledge bought a house for us (control). We lived together in that house for about two months. The last night we were together and after a one-sided argument, I went to bed with my shoes on because I was not allowed to leave the house with "his son." Instead of arguing with him, I thought it would be best for me to leave the house for a few hours, but he blocked the doorway and refused to let me leave. The next day, he left to go somewhere, and I snuck out of the house. This time, I had my son, his car seat, my car, laptop, and business cards (I was a loan officer at the time). I didn't pack any clothes because I didn't want him to catch me leaving. I went to my mother's and within two weeks, I moved from her house into a condo with my son and never looked back.

At that time, he told me that I was "a smart dumb bitch," and that I did not have shit and never would, and the only reason I did have anything was because of my daddy. He said that no one would want me and that I'd never find anyone like him. He was right, I never found anyone like him. That was in 2006.

There were many positive outcomes from this situation. For one, despite his behavior toward me, my son has no recollection of his father ever mistreating me. My child did not have to grow up witnessing his parents in an unhealthy relationship. Also, even though my son's current relationship with his dad is not ideal, they do have a communication channel, and the door remains open for them to build a stronger bond. If not, so be it.

Since 2006 (and maybe really my entire life), I've been on this journey of self-inquiry and discovery. I have also been on this quest for love and companionship which to this day, I have not found. A lot (maybe too many) of my reflections have to do with my dating life, which I recognize are both positive and negative.

I'm taking a chance by sharing my journal entries, but I figure that my story and thoughts may serve as a benefit to you as well as help me to transition into the next phase of my life, whatever that may be. I hope I'm right.

Your 1st Journal Entry

Owning Your Story: The Power of Storytelling

What is your backstory?

What life events marked the path for where you are today?

How have you displayed resilience?

Today's Date: _____

2nd JOURNAL ENTRY

Positive Affirmations

Solely focusing on the negative emotions and aspects of our lives increases our stress level and can drive some into a deeper depression and anxiety. The purpose of this guided journal is to help reverse those negative emotions. Yes? Well, let's make it a common practice to make positive statements about ourselves and our lives.

You can actually motivate yourself and manifest positive thoughts by writing personal messages to yourself and reciting them on a regular basis. Remember today's date. It's the date that you wrote your first positive affirmation to yourself in this journal. Once this journal is complete, reflect on this day and the time in between. You should feel more empowered.

Shawnta's 2nd Journal Entry

Positive Affirmations

I love the person that I am, and I love the person that I'm becoming. I'm strong enough to be weak and vulnerable, but tough enough to handle the things that come my way and wise enough to protect myself from false and negative people. I'm working on my mind and my spirit. I'm setting new standards and values for myself. I love myself.

I'm beautiful, inside out. I'm humble, sincere, fortunate, blessed, kind, and respectful. I respect others and I try to right my wrongs. I'm my father's daughter and my mother's child. I'm the descendant of my grandparents, their parents, and their parents. God bless them all. Bless their living spirits. I know that I make them proud and that I'm a reflection of them.

I'm at peace. I'm not perfect. I feel weak sometimes and I've made a lot of irresponsible and bad decisions in my life, and I don't like that I've put myself in certain situations, but I'm not going to hold these things against myself. God has kept me. He is protecting me and giving me his grace and mercy and I'm so thankful for that. I just pray that moving forward I don't repeat some of the same mistakes and decisions that I've made. I'm choosing not to be jaded by my experiences, especially my experiences with men. However, while I'm not jaded, I'm conscious and aware.

You're Shawnta Jackson! I'm Shawnta Jackson! Be proud, smile, and own it.

Your 2nd Journal Entry
Positive Affirmations

Be kind to yourself.

Be proud of yourself.

Remind yourself of who you really are or who you are aspiring to be.

Today's Date _____

Daily Practice: Write down three positive affirmations to yourself on a piece of paper. Read these positive affirmations out loud so that you can hear the words. Tape the piece of paper to your mirror or on your bathroom door.

3rd JOURNAL ENTRY

Expressions of Gratitude

According to a magazine article written by the famed clinical social worker, psychotherapist, and author, Amy Morin, seven scientifically proven benefits of gratitude can be explained as follows:[1]

1. Gratitude opens the door to more relationships.
2. Gratitude improves physical health.
3. Gratitude improves psychological health.
4. Gratitude enhances empathy and reduces aggression.
5. Grateful people sleep better.
6. Gratitude improves self-esteem.
7. Gratitude increases mental strength.

Additionally, I like to believe that gratitude also produces spiritual benefits such as continued blessings from God. Express gratitude and the universe will return it to you.

Shawnta's 3rd Journal Entry

Expressions of Gratitude

God is good to me. I'm grateful for God's guidance, visions, messages, and protection. I'm grateful that I'm able to provide for myself and for the resources available to me. I'm grateful that I'm able to understand, access, and use the resources available to me. I'm grateful for my knowledge, insight, and wisdom. I'm grateful that my mistakes have not ruined me. I'm grateful for God's forgiveness, mercy, and grace. I'm grateful for my son and my family. I'm grateful for my future family. I'm grateful to my ancestors and my descendants. I'm grateful for another day, another day of progress. I'm grateful for growth, peace, and sanity. I'm grateful for my mind and positivity. I ask that God remove negativity and negative and toxic people from my life.

May I have the wisdom to recognize these people and the courage to be okay with removing them from my life and keeping them at a distance. May I not judge people or be too hard on others or myself. I pray for unconditional love, unconditional internal love—unconditional love from my soulmate, the person who God has gifted me with to fulfill my destiny. I'm grateful for the man who compliments me and my purpose in life. I pray for spiritual health. As long as I have spiritual health, I have my mental and physical health because my spirit is just that amazing. I'm grateful. Amen.

Your 3rd Journal Entry
Expressions of Gratitude

Expressing gratitude improves your psychological health and creates reciprocity between you and God (also known as the Universe).

Write down at least five things that you are grateful for and why.

Today's Date _____

Expressions of Gratitude

Daily Practice: Write a second note to yourself on a piece of paper as a reminder to say what you're grateful for. Say it out loud so that you can hear yourself. Tape the note to your mirror or on your bathroom door next to your positive affirmations.

4th JOURNAL ENTRY

Manifesting Love

As humans, we are naturally wired to connect with one another. I've yet to meet a person who yearns for the feelings of loneliness and rejection. However, every person that I've ever met has sought and continues to seek this emotion and mental state that we call love. Regardless of your relationship status (married or single), I do believe that love is also intentional and can be manifested. Meaning that you have to make yourself available to give and receive love.

However, before we start journaling about manifesting love, it's important to have a true understanding of what love is and what love is not. Based on my personal research and experiences, love can be explained as follows:

1. Love is empathy and caring, not lust and infatuation.
2. Love is a verb, an action.
3. How we express love can be influenced by our culture, upbringing, and past experiences.
4. Love motivates people to care for others by trying to prevent or end their suffering.
5. Love is patient and kind and requires acceptance.
6. Love is not a fixed amount.
7. Love is communicated in different ways and we have to learn how we communicate our love and how our partner communicates their love. Love has languages.

Shawnta's 4th Journal Entry

Manifesting Love

I'm in tune with myself and I'm wise enough to recognize whether a person is right for me or not. I'm really good at spotting the "no's" but I'm working on opening my eyes to the "yes's."

I want love—true, sincere, unconditional love. Love for myself, love for him, love for each other, love for life, love for God, and love for those that both he and I love. I want respect, admiration, and attraction as well. Not just physical attraction. Attraction to his mind, his heart, his ways, the way he carries himself, how he treats others, and his thought processes.

Although he will have his own mind, he will think like me, he will lead me, carry me, and follow me too. I love him already and I don't think that we have met. If we have, my eyes and my heart have not opened to see or feel him. I just have to open up and let someone in but at the same time maintain respect for myself and my values. I'm done letting people take advantage of me, my time, my body, and my mind. He has to have self-respect and respect for me, my time, and my emotions. I'm trying my best to avoid selfish, insecure, and egotistical men.

Your 4th Journal Entry
Manifesting Love

Think about how you can love yourself better.

Whether you have a significant other or not, write how you want that person to love you. Reflect on the internal and external love you need to maintain a healthy relationship with yourself and the person you will share your life with.

Today's Date: _____

5th JOURNAL ENTRY

Expecting Love

Shawnta's 5th Journal Entry

Expecting Love

Yesterday, I said a blend of prayers, affirmations, and confirmations. I mainly focused on the fact that God is with me and that God is love. I'm love. I give love and receive love. I pray that I will be able to receive love from a man. I can accept love. The things that happened to me in the past were unfortunate, but they will not happen again. Plus, my experiences have helped make me the woman I am today. The person I am. The mother I am. I'm forgiving and I'm able to love unconditionally. I can't let my past experiences jeopardize my future. I tell myself, "Don't let your past stop you from experiencing love." This is my conscious feeding my subconscious because subconsciously, I'm not sure if I really believe in or expect love and true companionship.

Your 5th Journal Entry
Expecting Love

How do you feel about love?

How important is it for you to feel intimate love?

Describe how your past has positively or negatively affected your thoughts about love.

Be honest with yourself.

Today's Date: _____

Expecting Love

6th JOURNAL ENTRY

Self-Validation

In 2002, three well-known researchers published what has now been cited in over 600 research articles pertaining to self-validation. In their article, the researchers explain what they refer to as a self-validation hypothesis which basically states that the degree of confidence that people have in their own thoughts affects their self-validation. Positive thoughts increase our level of persuading ourselves which in my opinion leads to increased self-validation and lesser reliance on others to validate who we are and what we can achieve.[2]

Shawnta's 6th Journal Entry

Self-Validation

My personal plan for myself is to continue in the spiritual and mental direction that I'm going. I'm growing every day and every day God shows me a sign or delivers a message. Every day, I have communication with God. I appreciate my rising level of consciousness and spirituality.

My last day of being a permission-seeking person was September 18, 2018, but the day that I actually realized this was on September 30, 2018.

People gave me feedback on my presentation at a conference. While I appreciate the positive feedback, one person gave me feedback to help build my confidence. I realized that I had put it out there that I was nervous and unsure if the audience would be receptive to my words and this man picked up on that. At that moment, I knew that I was receiving the type of feedback and tips on public speaking and "being myself" because I invited that type of conversation by way of my energy and maybe body language.

What really made me realize that I did not need other people's validation was the fact that the person who gave me the feedback did not seem to be aware of his own lack of public speaking and facilitation skills. He was a very nice person and was knowledgeable, and I respect him and his position, but as I watched him speak, he lost me and other audience members during his keynote address. The point is, I provide good and appropriate information, and I connect with my audience. Yes, there is always room for improvement, and I welcome feedback, but I'm not seeking validation or approval and I have to be more conscious of my thoughts because other humans can pick up on the energy that I'm transmitting.

Your 6th Journal Entry
Self-Validation

Think about a time when you have or have not sought validation or approval from a person other than yourself.

Ask yourself if this is a pattern and if so, is it a healthy pattern?

Moving forward, what type of positive thoughts about who you are and your ability to achieve would you rather produce?

Today's Date: _____

7th JOURNAL ENTRY

Depending on a Power Greater Than Yourself

Whether you have a belief in only one God, no Gods at all, multiple Gods and Goddesses, Buddha, or the Universe, your spiritual and psychological well-being are connected and can positively or negatively impact your thoughts about yourself and how you choose to respond to those thoughts. According to many psychologists, believing in religion or a higher power fills the human need for finding meaning and purpose. These beliefs not only support us socially and culturally, but affect our inner selves, our mental strength, and mental capacity to experience life's challenges and come out healthy and sane.

Shawnta's 7th Journal Entry

Depending on a Power Greater Than Yourself

I was created by God and I have a purpose to live life abundantly, to seek wisdom and truth, and to help other people to do the same. Every vision, dream, or idea that I have comes from God, but it's up to me to accept and acknowledge God's guidance in the choices and actions that I make.

I pray for God to be with me. I pray for positive energy and positive manifestation. In fact, I've practiced positive manifestations. God has been and always will be with me, but at this point, He is so close, or should I say that I'm more aware? Yes. I'm more aware, conscious and I am more in tune with my own intuition which is all God. God is in me, God is with me, and it's a lot of power. A lot of energy. I welcome the energy. I welcome the intuition, the messages, and the visions, but it's a lot. I'm learning to channel my energy and to let go and go with the flow. I hear, I listen, and I say, "Okay." I'm humble. I'm grateful. I'm proud. I'm loved.

Your 7th Journal Entry
Depending on a Power Greater Than Yourself

To what extent do you believe in a power greater than yourself? How can you better align yourself with that power to co-create your life?

Today's Date: _____

8th JOURNAL ENTRY
Allowing yourself to Trust Someone Else

Before we can truly trust someone else, we must build enough confidence to trust and respect ourselves. We must trust ourselves to know that we have good judgment and the ability to make the best decisions for ourselves. We must set expectations and boundaries within and prioritize what is important to us. Once we do that, we will have a foundation.

We know who we are and what we expect out of relationships and interactions with people in general. If we build trust within, then we can have healthier relationships which consist of trust, communication, and respect.

Shawnta's 8th Journal Entry

Allowing Yourself to Trust Someone Else

I'm in tune with myself and I'm wise enough to recognize whether someone is or is not right for me. I'm really good at spotting the "no's," but I'm working on opening my eyes to the "yes's."

I tell myself, "Don't let your past stop you from experiencing love." I've trusted my life with someone before and even though the relationship did not work out, in the end, everything did work out and in my favor. I came out on top. I don't want to bring the past into the future, but is this possible? Is this where memory suppression begins?

The reason I don't remember what I experienced and how it affected me is because I was pretending. I was not telling myself the truth. When you lie to yourself, you forget those lies. I suffered through an unhealthy relationship and I don't want anyone else to experience what I did. Yes, there are those who have had it worse than me, but the long-term shame and abuse is detrimental to your mind and your self-esteem.

On the other hand, I'm grateful that there are a select few people who I can trust. Not everyone needs to know everything about me anyway. Not everyone can be trusted either. It's not because they are untrustworthy. Sometimes, it's because they are not worthy. Only soul connections should be allowed to know you on an intimate level. This does not have to be sexual either. For example, my friend Tya has a good spirit. We are connected and I trust and admire her.

Your 8th Journal Entry
Allowing Yourself to Trust Someone Else

Explain what trust means to you.

How easy or hard is it for you to trust someone else?

Think about the values of a trustworthy person and write down the names of the people who you can trust.

Also, write down the names of the people who can trust you.

What has this process revealed to you?

Today's Date: _____

9th JOURNAL ENTRY

Balancing Independence and Relationships

As humans and as adults, we should not depend on another person to "make" us happy. While people can contribute to our happiness, it is an individual responsibility. We should not be dependent on anyone to provide us with peace of mind or joy. While interdependence, such as depending on each other to maintain a home, lifestyle, or other goals is commendable, allowing yourself to be put in a position where you are unable as an adult to supply your own basic needs is not ideal, and in my opinion opens the door for control and even abuse. With that said, it's important for us all to find a healthy balance that works for our intimate relationships and for our individual selves.

Shawnta's 9th Journal Entry

Balancing Independence and Relationships

Everyone in my family is "independent." Independent and single. That can be seen as a positive thing, but I don't see it that way. I know that I can live the rest of my life as a single and dating person and achieve much success and be okay in life. I know this. I'm actually comfortable not sharing my space and making life decisions on my own.

However, I don't want to be so independent that I'm not capable of being in a relationship and sharing my life with someone. That being said, I do want to be loved. I do want to receive and accept love and reciprocate that love. I just have to allow myself to give it a chance and not run or push that person away out of fear. The last guy that I dated told me that I was a runner. That may be true, but I realized that he was a person that I should have run from in the beginning. He was not worthy of my time, my person. He was not and is not the one. I have no doubt in my mind about that. I made the right decision to stop dating him. I guess that is one of the perks of being independent. You don't feel like you have to put up with a person who is truly not for you.

Your 9th Journal Entry
Balancing Independence and Relationships

When it comes to relationships and your independence, what do you know to be true about yourself?

Give yourself advice.

Today's Date: _____

10th JOURNAL ENTRY

Unconditional Love and Commitment

Unconditional love can be described as feeling affection for someone regardless of life's circumstances. What unconditional love is not is feeling affection for someone regardless of the way they treat you. There is such a thing as loving someone from a distance.

As for commitment, according to researchers, commitment has two elements: personal dedication and constraint commitment.[3] Basically, dedication versus obligation.

Personal dedication is an individual's desire to maintain or improve the quality of a relationship for the benefit of both parties. While with constraint commitment, there are forces that constrain you and make you maintain a relationship regardless of your personal desires or dedication.[3]

Shawnta's 10th Journal Entry

Unconditional Love and Commitment

I think I have it wrong. Instead of focusing on whether or not I can receive love, the real questions are: Can I love someone? Can I unconditionally love someone? Can I fall in love? Can I commit to one person? Maybe I've put up a wall, and maybe I'm scared of commitment. No, I'm not afraid to commit, I'm afraid of choosing the wrong person. Yes, I absolutely can love someone unconditionally, but I can't force feelings on myself that are not genuine and I'm afraid that is what will happen if I'm not careful and honest with myself.

Your 10th Journal Entry
Unconditional Love and Commitment

Describe what it means to you to unconditionally love someone.

What happens when you unconditionally love the wrong person or is there such a thing? Have you ever been in that situation? If so, what was the outcome?

Today's Date: _____

11th JOURNAL ENTRY

Shallow Thinking

Shallow thinking is looking at only what is on the surface, what we see, what satisfies us for the moment. Shallow thinking arguably aligns with instant gratification. We want things the way we want them, and we want them right away with minimal effort. Shallow thinkers are also known to be materialistic and pretentious. Pretentious people pretend and are attracted to people who appear to be important or talented.

The opposite of shallow thinking is deep thinking. It is looking at the bigger picture and exploring ways to make things work. Deep thinkers process and consider the short-term, medium-term, and long-term outcomes. Deep thinkers take the time to know and appreciate people for who they really are and not what they appear to be or what we want them to be.

While being shallow has a connotation of producing negative outcomes, thinking too deep can take the fun out of life. Whichever way you think, the goal is to be more conscious of your thoughts and recognize when the way you are thinking starts hindering your relationships or potential relationships.

Shawnta's 11th Journal Entry

Shallow Thinking

It's a competitive world out there and I should not force myself to be with someone I'm not physically attracted to or someone who does not maintain his personal appearance. That's what it really is. I may be shallow, but maybe not. I want my man to be well put together. That's what's attractive to me. I'm not talking about a playboy that only wears designer clothing either. I'm talking about someone who cares about his personal appearance.

Men want us to look good all the time, so I don't see why I can't be with a man who maintains a fresh haircut and shave? A nice haircut goes a long way. As for clothes, I know that I can make fashion recommendations. I'm not trying to be shallow and I don't think that requiring a man to have wrinkle-free, fuzz-free, and well-fitting clothing is asking for too much. I don't want to look at a homely looking man.

Men take women shopping all the time or upgrade a woman's wardrobe by buying gifts, but I don't want to be a person who makes a man feel like I'm trying to change him. I don't want to be the mean girl even though I've had no problem doing so in the past. I want my man to be who he is. However, if he's a homely looking man, I will not be confident and happy with him.

Your 11th Journal Entry
Shallow Thinking

When choosing who to associate with or who to date, do you have a history of thinking shallow or deep?

What about now?

Write down the pros and cons of both forms of thought and how they may help or hinder the types of relationships that you choose to form.

Today's Date: _____

12th JOURNAL ENTRY

Staying True to Yourself

You're entitled to live the single life and reject what does not feel right to you. You're entitled to decide where you stand in a relationship, who you want to be in a relationship with, and why or why not. In my opinion, taking a stance on your relationship status, the type of relationship, and who you choose to be in a relationship with begins with determining your self-worth, standards, and desired quality of life. Working to improve your level of emotional intelligence is also beneficial.

Emotional intelligence is when you have an understanding of emotions. Emotionally intelligent people have the ability to not only assess and manage their own emotions but are also able to assess the emotions of others and respond accordingly. Emotional intelligence helps you make better decisions about dating and relationships, including being true and honest with yourself and assessing how you feel about certain situations and those who have the ability to affect your happiness and quality of life.

Shawnta's 12th Journal Entry

Staying True to Yourself

I want to be healthy, independent, and successful. I am those things now, but I have not reached my ultimate level. Can I be independent and successful and still be in a healthy and rewarding relationship? Yes! I don't want to give up my dreams to be with a man. So far, it seems like every guy that I've met means giving up on my dreams in order to be in a fairy-tale relationship. There are exceptions of course, but it seems like I can't win for losing. No, I take that back. I'm winning. I'm able to stay true to myself, even if that means losing people or being alone. I'm not picky, I'm me. I have standards and I need to learn to follow those standards in all situations, no matter what. I know how to be flexible and nurturing. That's who I am as a human being.

I'm sitting at home at my dining room table. I cooked dinner and I'm eating while watching YouTube motivational videos. There is so much on my mind and so many things that I want to write about, but I can't seem to figure out in which order.

For the past few days, I've been debating if I want to be in a relationship with this guy or not. The answer is "no." I don't mind dating him but I'm not ready to be in a relationship with him; and to be honest, I'm not sure if I will ever want to be in a relationship with him. He is a nice guy, but I don't see myself being happy in the life that I imagine with him. I could be totally wrong, but I am not going to force myself into a situation or relationship. He wants a traditional marriage and kids. For a minute, I went along with the idea and convinced myself that I wanted the same or at least I tried to convince myself, but it didn't work.

I have dreams and a vision for myself and feel like I shouldn't have to choose and let go of some of the things I hoped to do in life. Plus, I would not be happy living in the type of community that he wants us to live in. Also, I don't know if I can fall in love with him. I don't know if I'd be happy with only him which is why he and I should not be in a relationship—at least not at the moment. Honestly, I don't think that he and I will ever be, and I'm okay with that, too.

I'm really glad that I have decided to abstain from sex because I don't feel bad about myself or hate myself.

Your 12th Journal Entry
Staying True to Yourself

What are the pros and cons of being single?

What type of relationship or relationships do you have now?

Does it (or do they) align with your self-worth, standards, and desired quality of life? Moving forward, what should you be more mindful of when it comes to relationships and your happiness?

Today's Date: _____

13th JOURNAL ENTRY

Managing Anxiety and Stress

As I mentioned previously, journaling has healthy benefits. As you will see in my journal entry below, sometimes a quick note to yourself about what's on your mind which is causing anxiety and stress can provide instant relief or at least clarity.

Other than journaling, additional activities that can help you manage or prevent anxiety or feeling overwhelmed are:

- Meditation
- Deep breathing
- Physical activity
- Listening to music
- Comedies
- Confiding in or venting to a trusted person
- Developing a "to do" list
- Learning to say "no" or "no, not right now" or "no, I don't have it to give"
- Love people from a distance
- Turn off your phone notifications
- Don't compare yourself to others

Shawnta's 13th Journal Entry

Managing Anxiety and Stress

I have a few things on my mind. I'm writing tonight for clarity. If I'm not careful, I'll become overwhelmed and anxious. The last thing I want to do is tell God that I can't handle it and not receive any more blessings. I just need to remind myself that God is with me and guiding me. I can only do so much in one day.

"Trust in the Lord with all your heart and lean not on your own understanding; in all your ways acknowledge Him, and He shall direct your paths" Proverbs 3:5-6. Wow, Amen. I needed to read this verse. Amen. God is always sending me messages right when I need them. God bless me. I'm very thankful.

I will not complain. I'll accept things for what they are and deal with them accordingly. For every problem, there is a solution.

Your 13th Journal Entry
Managing Anxiety and Stress

What are some of the things that are on your mind that can potentially cause you stress or anxiety?

Think it out and come to a conclusion as to how you can best handle these things moving forward.

Do you need to change your mind-set in order to gain clarity?

Today's Date: _____

14th JOURNAL ENTRY

Your Relationship with Time and Money

There are three main ways to use time and money. You can waste it, save it, or invest it. Both time and money are limited resources and are most beneficial when you receive a return on your investment, which doesn't always equate to material things or other monetary values. These returns can be more money and time to spend on the things that you truly value, such as family time, leisure activities, and self-development. Whatever your outcomes are presently, and in the future, they are most likely the result of your relationship with either time, money or both.

For example, if you spend your time on drama, dysfunction, and mindless television, this is what your life outcomes will reflect. The same is true with money. Money is a tool, a resource that impacts our overall wellness. While money may not buy happiness, mismanaging money or not having enough money can affect our stress level and if misused can cost us more in the long run in the form of higher interest rates, loss of possessions, and an unhealthy amount of debt.

Shawnta's 14th Journal Entry

Your Relationship with Time and Money

Money is not my end goal. I see money as a resource that I need to pay my bills and live life. Money will help me to reach my fullest potential and to continue growing. One thing that I need to work on is limiting the amount of money that I spend. If my goal is to reduce my personal debt and start investing in real estate to build my retirement portfolio, I need to be more disciplined and intentional about how I utilize cash and credit. Another thing that I need to work on is limiting my time on social media. It's a distraction, and the majority of the time it is mostly negative or mindless comments and posts. By not allowing notifications from my social media and email accounts, I avoid unnecessary distractions. I also find that my days are more productive if I avoid directing my attention toward social media first thing in the morning. Instead, I try to feed and stimulate my mind with information via motivational speeches, music, business content, or a book.

Your 14th Journal Entry
Your Relationship with Time and Money

What is your relationship with money?

What mistakes and amendments have you made, or do you need to make?

Are there things about money management that you feel you need help with?

What about your time?

How does the way that you utilize your time impact your current situation?

What are you going to do about it?

Today's Date: _____

_____
_____
_____
_____
_____
_____
_____
_____
_____
_____
_____
_____
_____
_____
_____
_____
_____

15th JOURNAL ENTRY

Spontaneous Thoughts

Just because you randomly think about or say things, it doesn't mean that you should dismiss those thoughts. Not everything has to be planned and be in a particular order. Not every journal entry has to have a theme. Sometimes, you just might want to think and write freely. Remember, your journal entries mean that you are being true to yourself. It's your journal and you can do what you want to with it.

Shawnta's 15th Journal Entry

Spontaneous Thoughts

These are my moments. I've thought about disposing this journal like I've done in the past, but I'm not going to do that with this one. I've been asking a lot of questions about myself, and yesterday I reread some of my entries. I'm sometimes embarrassed by myself, but oh well. I am who I am.

I amaze myself, too. I'm a really good person and I'm dedicated. I'm dedicated to my son. I will do whatever I can to find the resources to help him excel and exceed in life. I'm grateful that I am able to support him. I'm grateful that God allows me to support him mentally, provide security, and love him unconditionally. I am grateful that I have been able to protect my son from abuse, neglect, negativity, and so on. Yes, he must deal with things socially, but he has a safe and healthy home.

I'm grateful for my family. My parents are good people and I'm blessed to have them in my life. I have to do a better job of not taking my mother for granted. Lately, I've been busy when she has called, and I failed to give her my full attention.

I love me. I love my personality. I'm such a character and I'm outgoing. I think I'm pretty funny and usually it's not intentional.

I've been really lazy lately, too. For example, I'm still in bed even though I have things to do and it is 10:40 am. It seems like I always have something to do though. I'm not complaining, I'm just acknowledging that I need to get my priorities straight. I need to clean and organize my life. I still haven't set goals for the year, personal or business. I need to start working out, too. I feel like I need a makeover. I need a new boost of swag or something. I'm thinking about cutting my hair.

Your 15th Journal Entry
Spontaneous Thoughts

Write whatever comes to your mind.

Today's Date: _____

Spontaneous Thoughts

16th JOURNAL ENTRY

Life in the Present Moment

Life is now. If you spend too much of your time dwelling in the past or thinking about the future, you're missing out on what is real at the moment. While we all think about the past and fantasize about the future—being present in the moment is your reference point for what is actually occurring in your life now, how you feel about it, and will help you identify those areas that can use improvement. Living in the moment not only helps you to take inventory of your life presently, this practice also helps to build your level of self-awareness, appreciation, emotional intelligence, and authenticity.

Shawnta's 16th Journal Entry

Life in the Present Moment

Hello, world. I'm here. I'm present. I give and receive positive energy. I grow and thrive from my interactions with others. I see potential in myself and in others. I am able to read people and that's okay. I understand their stories. This is life. We are life.

My life—the type of life that I have, the type of life that I live. I have the freedom to do as I please. This means that I can decide how I spend my day—at least for the most part. When I have appointments, that's a different story, but even then, I choose my schedule and agree to meeting times.

Freedom—I am able to travel and can pretty much work from anyplace in the world. I parent—I love doing things for my son and keeping him involved in activities. I'm writing this poolside on the rooftop of a condo building in Thailand. My life is good, but I'm not comfortable. I'm not where I want to be. I want to continue and maintain what I'm doing and grow in the process. I'm not where I want to be.

Where I want to be—the lifestyle I want to live, the things I want to accomplish, the person I must become to get there, the things I must do, and the next best step. It's important for me to remind myself of what I want, and it is also an opportunity to decide if I want to adjust or change my mind.

Your 16th Journal Entry
Life in the Present Moment

Think about the conversations that you have had with yourself and others.

Do you spend most of your thoughts or conversation on past experiences, what is going on now in your life, or on what the future may look like?

Write about you and your life in the present moment.

How do you feel about now?

Date: _____

17th JOURNAL ENTRY

Life Visioning

Life is about growth and change, and in my opinion, the best life lived is when you are intentional about growing and changing by creating a vision for your life. Yes, it's important to live in the moment, but creating a vision can help you map out your path to achieving your life's goals. It can assist you in determining what needs to be done and who you must become to make your vision a reality.

Your vision for life may change over time and when it does, you can re-imagine your path and how you will get there. Your vision should embody your values and standards whether it is family, love, health, wealth, spirituality, career, freedom, independence, or all of the above. Your vision should serve as your source for inspiration. When times get tough, your vision should be a reminder of why you chose this path and what you are working toward. Your vision is also a way of manifesting what is to come.

Shawnta's 17th Journal Entry

Life Visioning

I would definitely like a life partner, but I'm not sure when or how that will happen. It would be great to have someone to dream and work on life goals with. Companionship is important and I will have that someone, but in the meantime, I'm going to continue to plan and live my life accordingly. I will just have to be patient and understand that I have a great life to live and will only continue to grow. When the time is right, I will meet someone that will promote my personal, spiritual, mental, physical, and professional growth. We will complement one another, and he will not be a hindrance or prevent me from excelling.

I want to continue to travel the world and explore God's creations and wonders. I want to teach people what I know and expose my son to the world and its opportunities.

I want to develop a real estate portfolio of rental properties in the United States and internationally. As I did last summer and as I'll be doing this summer, God willing, I will be traveling with my son and working from remote locations within or even outside of the United States. I would like to spend a summer in a Spanish-speaking country to learn the language.

As far as living, I think I want to own condos. I wouldn't mind having a nice sized home with a driveway, foyer, and backyard, but then again, I don't want to commit myself to too much maintenance and responsibility. Maybe when I have a husband that will be different.

I definitely don't want to be in a lot of debt. I want financial freedom and very little out-of-pocket expenses. I'd like to travel with my parents as well. Maybe I can take them somewhere in the fall or at the end of the year.

Your 17th Journal Entry
Life Visioning

If you had the option to design your life for the next two to five years or for a lifetime, what would it look like?

What would you be doing and with whom?

What type of lifestyle would you live?

What type of person would you be?

Date: _____

Life Visioning Activity: In addition to writing your life vision in this journal, I encourage you to buy a poster board and get some old magazines or search the Internet for words and pictures that depict your vision. Using those words and pictures, create a vision board and place it on the wall in your bedroom or other place of choice. In addition to saying your words of gratitude and positive affirmations, on occasion, review this board to motivate yourself to keep working toward your vision. If you don't want to create your vision board alone, invite a few friends to join you and make it a party.

18th JOURNAL ENTRY

Another Expression of Gratitude

As I mentioned at the beginning of this journal, expressing gratitude helps to improve your mental health and creates reciprocity between you and God also known as the Universe. Expressing gratitude is also known to:

1. Open the door to more relationships
2. Improve your physical health
3. Enhance your empathy and reduce aggression
4. Help you sleep better
5. Improve your self-esteem
6. Help increase your mental strength

Shawnta's 18th Journal Entry

Another Expression of Gratitude

Hello, world. I'm thirty-eight years old now. I just read some of my entries and once again I feel embarrassed. I realize that this isn't the first time that I have said this—I wonder what a psychologist would say if they read my journal entries. I wonder what my son and my parents would think.

Side Note: I really, really need to work out. I'm going to have to go on a strict diet and exercise regiment because my midsection is out of control.

Okay. Now that I'm finished bashing myself, I can talk about the things that I'm grateful for. I'm grateful for every day I have on this earth and my future. I'm grateful for the positive and supportive people that God has brought into my life.

I am building a network, my network. My son is respectful and doesn't really give me any problems. I'm grateful for that as well. I'm grateful that I am able to provide for myself and my son. I'm grateful for my health. I'm grateful for my heart. I'm grateful that I am still open to love.

I'm getting closer to achieving my next big accomplishment. Exactly what it will be, I don't know, but I work hard and commit to every project that I work on. I'm grateful for this as well.

Your 18th Journal Entry
Another Expression of Gratitude

At the moment, what are you most grateful for?

Date: _____

Another Expression of Gratitude

Daily Practice Reminder: On a piece of paper write a note to reminding yourself to say those things that you are grateful for. Say these out loud so that you can hear yourself. Tape the note to your mirror or on your bathroom door next to your positive affirmations.

19th JOURNAL ENTRY

Striving for Success

Simply put, striving for success means putting forth strenuous effort toward a goal. The key word is *strenuous*, meaning a lot of hard effort. You must be consistent in this effort and expect there to be highs and lows—and expect to learn and grow through trial and error.

It has been said many times that success is not an accident. Like anything else worth achieving, success is intentional. Success is mapped out. Success is planned to the best of your ability. In order to achieve what you deem your success to be you need to have an idea and a plan as to how you will get there.

Shawnta's 19th Journal Entry

Striving for Success

Tomorrow is sort of a big day for me. I will be hosting my company's first-quarter webinar. I always get nervous and feel pressured when there are so many people listening to me while also managing technology and engaging with the audience. All will be well though. I will not worry. I have a good guest presenter as well as my intern to help.

I just have to keep going and taking action. I'm in the middle of growth. I'm in the midst of success. It's in progress. I know it. It's near but it is still so strange. It will be something that I could never fathom. I'm grateful for it even if it hasn't happened yet.

I've been thinking a lot about my show lately, too. I have also been thinking about which of my guest speakers I should have and the topics I want to cover. My audience will be people who are open to being more socially conscious and who want to understand how our lives are intertwined and affect one another. My goal is for my audience to learn about the social determinants of health, health equity, social justice issues, as well as expose them to people and organizations who advocate and provide human services. My guests will include thought leaders, influencers, advocates, educators, public health professionals, and everyday people.

Your 19th Journal Entry
Striving for Success

Think about what success means to you.

Write down your idea of success for yourself.

What does it look like?

What are the best next steps that you need to take in order to get closer to success?

Date: _____

_____
_____
_____
_____
_____
_____
_____
_____
_____
_____
_____
_____
_____
_____
_____
_____
_____
_____
_____

20th JOURNAL ENTRY

Perseverance

As you and I already know, not every day is a good day. You will doubt yourself. You will have thoughts of giving up, but the key is to allow yourself to process those feelings and not allow those thoughts sway you as you strive to move forward.

Giving up is one of the easiest things to do. That's why so many people do it. However, you are not most people. You are emotionally strong, intelligent, and aware. You know that these moments of self-doubt are temporary and that you will persevere.

Shawnta's 20th Journal Entry

Perseverance

Today, I feel down. Not at my lowest point but just low energy. I need to refocus on what it is that I want to achieve. I have completed my business planning for the year and my quarterly goals, but I'm still not doing everything that I need to do. I feel like I need to isolate myself from social media and friends for a while. It is not like I have a lot of friends, but I'm not committing as much time as I should to growing my business.

I need to further develop my niche and focus on a target audience that seeks my services. An audience that needs my assistance.

I know it is not healthy, emotionally strong, or the right thing to do, but lately I've been comparing where I am in life and in business to others. I know that my time will come but I feel like I'm doing something wrong. I can do it, but I'm tired of doing it by myself. No more complaints.

Your 20th Journal Entry
Perseverance

Think about a time when you had to persevere through a challenging time.

What got you through it?

What advice would you give to your future self when facing tough times or times of doubt and confusion?

Date: _____

21st JOURNAL ENTRY

Life's Bucket List

Most people define a bucket list as a list of things someone wants to do before they die, but not me—I'm not thinking about death. I define my bucket list as a list of things that I want to do in the near future. As I check things off my bucket list, I'll continue to add more. This gives me something to live for other than work and being a mother.

Shawnta's 21st Journal Entry

Life's Bucket List

- Go-go dance for one night at a nightclub in a popular city
- Stand-up comedy for one night
- Singing lessons
- Host my own TV show
- Preach a sermon
- Write a book
- Fall in love on a boat in the Mediterranean
- Visit Yellowstone Park
- Travel the world collecting handmade and custom jewelry
- Tour museums and historic sites of Ethiopia
- A summer road trip across the United States in an RV

Your 21st Journal Entry
Life's Bucket List

Don't worry about how you're going to do it or if you have the means to do it right now. Don't limit yourself.

What are some things in life that you have always wanted to do?

Create your own bucket list and dare yourself to start checking things off.

Date: _____

Dear Reader,

Thank you for taking the time to read my personal journal entries and for participating in this process. I'm curious to know what you think about this guided journal and if and how it has helped you. Please share your thoughts by emailing me at: shawnta@shawntajackson.com.

I would also like to see your positive affirmations, vision boards, and bucket lists. If you tag me on Instagram or Facebook @TheShawntaJackson, or Twitter @ShawntaTweets, with your photos and videos using the hashtag #journalingwithshawnta, I'll repost your testimonials and add them to my website at: www.ShawntaJackson.com.

Your Friend,

Shawnta Jackson

ABOUT THE AUTHOR

Shawnta Jackson is that person who leaves a lasting impression. She motivates, challenges, and provides thought provoking solutions. She is a leader, mother, and social entrepreneur with a vision to help people help themselves and others.

In addition to writing, Shawnta helps organizations across the United States to plan, implement, and share the outcomes of their socially conscious initiatives. She also serves as a facilitator and guest speaker for various audiences.

She holds a Master of Public Health degree in social and behavioral health from University of Nevada, Las Vegas, and a Bachelor of Arts degree in public relations from Columbia College Chicago.

Shawnta resides in the Washington-Baltimore metropolitan area with her son, Zachary.

REFERENCES

3rd Journal Entry: Expressions of Gratitude

1   Morin, Amy. "7 Scientifically Proven Benefits of Gratitude." *Psychology Today*. April 3, 2015. Accessed December 10, 2019. https://www.psychologytoday.com/us/blog/what-mentally-strong-people-dont-do/201504/7-scientifically-proven-benefits-gratitude

6th Journal Entry: Self-Validation

2   Petty, Richard E., Pablo Briñol, and Zachary L. Tormala. "Thought confidence as a determinant of persuasion: The self-validation hypothesis." *Journal of Personality and Social Psychology* 82, no. 5 (2002): 722-741. doi.org/10.1037/0022-3514.82.5.722.

10th Journal Entry: Unconditional Love and Commitment

3   Stanley, Scott M., and Howard J. Markman. "Assessing Commitment in Personal Relationships." *Journal of Marriage and Family* 54, no. 3 (1992): 595-608. doi:10.2307/353245.